PLANETS

For Conor

Pushkin Press
Somerset House, Strand
London WC2R 1LA

Planets was first published by Pushkin Press in 2022
This edition published 2025

1 3 5 7 9 8 6 4 2

ISBN 978-1-78269-521-9

Cover design by John Devolle

Printed and bound in China by C&C Offset Printing Co Ltd

www.pushkinpress.com

PLANETS

By John Devolle

Pushkin Children's Books

Hello!

**Maybe you are sitting at home thinking
'It's pretty boring where I live'…**

But you'd be wrong, because right now you are spinning at over 600 miles per hour as the Earth (where you live) turns on its axis!

The Earth is also hurtling around the Sun at 67,000 miles per hour.
One trip around the Sun is 584 million miles long and takes 365 days.
That's what we call a year.

It's amazing that you don't fall off!

But the Earth is just
one of the planets
that make up our
solar system.

There are seven other
planets all travelling
around the Sun at
different speeds.

So let's see if it might be more fun to live on another planet, shall we?

We'll need a rocket and a lot of energy to break free of our Earth's gravity. That's what we call the force that pulls everything down towards the ground and stops us all floating up into the sky.

The smallest and closest planet to our Sun is Mercury.

The half of the planet facing the Sun is much too hot and the other half, in the shade, is much too cold.

How about Venus?

Well, it is covered in volcanoes spewing out horrible, eggy, sulphurous smoke.

Or perhaps Mars? It has a rocky, red surface and is the most similar planet to our own…

But there isn't much gravity on Mars. If you tried to eat your dinner there it would get very messy!

Then there's Jupiter.

It's the biggest planet in our solar system.

The 'Great Red Spot' you can see is actually a huge storm, wider than the Earth, that has been raging ever since it was first seen 350 years ago.

Oooooooo, Saturn looks nice doesn't it, with its lovely rings?

Unfortunately, the rings are actually made up of rocks and ice, and the planet is just swirling gases with nothing solid to land on, let alone live on!

Ah, Uranus. At last, a solid surface.
But it's the coldest planet in the solar system.
Temperatures reach as low as -224 degrees Celsius.
That's **T-T-T-TOOOOO C-C-C-COLD!**

Now we are right at the edge of our solar system on Neptune. We're a very long way from the Sun.

Neptune takes so long to go around the Sun that a year here is 164.8 times longer than on Earth. If you lived here, you'd only have a birthday once every 164.8 Earth years!

So let's go back home, shall we?

Because…
of all these
planets there's
only one that's
just the right size,
just the right
distance from the
Sun, which is just
big enough to
give just enough
heat and energy
to support life
in all its many
forms.

And that's the Earth.

WHAT ABOUT PLUTO?!!!
Pluto is so small and
far away from the Sun that it's
no longer considered a planet
and has been reclassified
as a 'dwarf planet'.